to a Christian Nation:
Counter Point

Letter
to a Christian Nation:
Counter Point

R.C. Metcalf

iUniverse, Inc.
New York Lincoln Shanghai

Letter to a Christian Nation: Counter Point

iUniverse books may be ordered through booksellers or by contacting:

iUniverse
2021 Pine Lake Road, Suite 100
Lincoln, NE 68512
www.iuniverse.com
1-800-Authors (1-800-288-4677)

ISBN-13: 978-0-595-43264-6 (pbk)
ISBN-13: 978-0-595-87605-1 (ebk)
ISBN-10: 0-595-43264-6 (pbk)
ISBN-10: 0-595-87605-6 (ebk)

Printed in the United States of America

The views expressed in this work are solely those of the author and do not necessarily reflect the views of the publisher, and the publisher hereby disclaims any responsibility for them.

For my beloved wife

Contents

NOTE TO THE READER

SAM HARRIS' recent bestseller *Letter to a Christian Nation* merits an intelligent response that offers the reader a rationale for the credibility and rectitude of orthodox Christianity. Not all individuals who claim to be Christians fully exemplify the moral teachings of Jesus. In fact, many by their words and actions cast a shadow on the name of Christ. Nevertheless, millions of intelligent Christians in America have thoughtfully compared their Christian faith with atheism and found the latter consistently lacking in both evidence and any real foundational warrant for moral integrity. This does not suggest that atheists cannot be moral people or live moral lives, only that they have nothing on which to ground their morality. Atheism provides society with no inherent basis upon which to distinguish between right and wrong other than by popular consensus, and few would suggest that the majority is always correct.

As one "transformed by Christ's love"[1] but not "deeply, even murderously, intolerant of criticism,"[2] this treatise will prove useful to all readers as a presentation of a reasoned defense of protestant, orthodox, evangelical Christianity. Please understand at the outset that terms like "orthodox," "protestant," and "catholic"[3] have specific meanings in their own right, prior to their adoption by certain religious sects. By "orthodox" I simply mean, that which adheres to essential doctrines of the Christian church as they have been defined and defended since the time of Christ. By "protestant" I am referring to those branches of Christianity that arose as a result of the 16th-century Reformation, initiated by Martin Luther in 1517 and perpetuated by men such as Calvin, Zwingli and Knox. The Reformation was a protest against the corruption of the established Roman Catholic Church at the time. Since the Reformation, protestant believers have united in their rejection of the authority of the Pope, but have disaffiliated due to doctrinal nuances considered non-essential when compared with the core teachings of orthodox Christianity. The teachings of Islam, Judaism, Buddhism, Hinduism and virtually all other faiths differ markedly from orthodox Christianity. A consistent error in Harris' writing, as well as in the writing of Richard Dawkins[4], is the tendency to categorize all faiths under the rubric of "religion," thereby blurring the doctrinal distinctions between them.

For most of the 500 years that preceded the Reformation, the Roman Catholic Church was the majority representative of Christianity. The 11th century saw the Great Schism between the Roman Catholic Church and the Eastern Orthodox Church, in which the Eastern Church denounced the Pope's alteration of the Nicene Creed without the consent of an ecumenical council. The Roman papacy sanctioned the horrors of the Crusades and the Spanish Inquisition that Harris places on the shoulders of generic "Christianity." The Spanish Inquisition, although initially focused on false converts to the Roman Church from Judaism and Islam in the late 1400s, eventually turned its focus toward Protestant Christians subsequent to the Reformation.

Protestants like John Calvin and Martin Luther seem to adopt different personalities that vary according to the point of view of the biographer. Harris claims that "John Calvin advocated the wholesale murder of heretics, apostates, Jews, and witches,"[5] which he presumably discovered from William Manchester's book *A World Lit Only by Fire*.[6] Contrary to this view, the historian Kenneth Scott Latourette states that "in spite of Calvin's plea [to the civil authorities] for a more merciful form of execution, Servetus was burned at the stake …"[7] In fact, Michael Servetus was the only individual executed in

xiv   *Letter to a Christian Nation: Counter Point*

Geneva during Calvin's lifetime, during an era when such executions were commonplace elsewhere.[8] Regardless of the difference of opinion between these two historians, the vast majority of the brutality perpetrated historically, in the name of Christ, has resulted from the turpitudes of the early Roman Catholic Church, not protestant Christianity. In mid-sixteenth century England, Mary I, of the Tudor dynasty, also known as "Bloody Mary," executed Protestants in an effort to return England to Roman Catholicism. During her brief five year reign she ordered the deaths of over 280 Protestant Christians, many more than those executed in any five year period during the Spanish Inquisition. Mary I was responsible for the executions of many notable reformers, such as Thomas Cranmer, Hugh Latimer, Nicholas Ridley and John Bradford.

In America today, there are approximately twice the number of evangelical Protestant Christians as there are Roman Catholic adherents.[9] Worldwide, the Roman Catholic Church has made great strides to repair some of the rifts that previously existed. In 1964, Pope Paul VI met with the Eastern Orthodox leader, Ecumenical Patriarch Athenagoras I, and rescinded the anathemas of the Great Schism of 1054. A similar attempt at ecumenism occurred with the 1994 release of the document Evangelicals and

Catholics Together, drafted by Charles Colson and Fr. John Neuhaus. Both of these attempts at reconciliation met with some legitimate dissent, due to distinct doctrinal differences, yet neither event yielded acts of violence such as those perpetrated historically or by extremist adherents of Islam today.

In the final analysis, true Christian believers are found in the Roman Catholic Church as well as protestant churches today. Conversely, many from both churches claim the name of Christ but do not truly represent Him, as both Mr. Harris and Richard Dawkins found from letters they received. Jesus amplifies this truth in Matthew 13:24-30, commonly known as the Parable of the Wheat and the Tares. In three of the four gospels Jesus asks Peter, "Who do you say I am?" This question cries out for a response from everyone alive today, because the correct answer results in a life forever changed, in a very positive direction, by the grace of God.

Harris claims to address Christians in a very narrow sense, as persons who believe, "at a minimum, that the Bible is the inspired word of God and that only those who accept the divinity of Jesus Christ will experience salvation after death."[10] Yet as one reads his book, it becomes patently obvious that these are not the only two doctrines of Christianity under attack. In *Letter to a Christian Nation*, Harris sets out "to demolish the intellectual and moral pretensions of Christianity in its most committed forms."[11] In response, I will be directing my comments to Mr. Harris and to any readers who may find his arguments persuasive. A "pretension" is an unsupportable claim. Yet, is Christianity truly unsupportable? Or does good, cogent, intellectual, historical, philosophical and even scientific evidence exist to support Christianity?

Harris points out that a recent Gallup poll "revealed that 53 percent of Americans are actually creationists."[12] He then goes on to say that "this means that despite a full century of scientific insights attesting to the antiquity of life and the greater antiquity of the earth, more than half our neighbors believe that the entire cosmos was created six thousand years ago."[13] He fails to mention that among those Christians who believe that God created the earth, there exist at least two camps, young earth creationists and old earth creationists. While hotly disputed among Christians, one's opinion regarding the age of the earth is classified as a non-essential concept that falls outside the realm of foundational Christian doctrine. While both camps believe that God "created" the cosmos, and hence would consider themselves creationists, they do not both adhere to a six thousand year age for the cosmos. By reading the poll in such a way as to equate *creationists* with specifically *young earth creationists,*

Harris commits the logical fallacy of equivocation. Many of the Americans who took the survey probably did not perceive the term *creationist* to mean *young earth creationist*.

Remember also that Americans of other faiths may well believe in some form of creation. Granted, most other faiths comprise a smaller portion of the American population than Christians, but their participation would skew the statistics slightly. For example, most Sunni Muslims would generally classify themselves as creationists, but adhere to an Islamic form of evolutionary creationism. Therefore, most Sunni Muslims would not believe that the entire cosmos was created six thousand years ago. Sunni Muslims represent the majority of Muslims in America, just as in the rest of the world.[14]

Statistics have long been intentionally misused to interpret data in ways that make the results appear favorable to the presenter. Harris either intentionally allies himself with this dubious tradition of statistical invalidity or simply fails to see the impact of the unstated factors that skew the results in his favor. Claiming to understand clearly what "we believe"[15] Harris proceeds to pronounce judgment upon us for those beliefs. Unfortunately, his understanding of our beliefs seems just as skewed as his statistics.

Mr. Harris claims that "the primary purpose of [his] book is to arm secularists in our society, who believe that religion should be kept out of public policy, against their opponents on the Christian Right."[16] Conversely, I propose to offer Christians a response to secularists who have been so armed. However, regardless of its effect on public policy, it remains my sincere desire that this book will provide the reader, along with Mr. Harris, a clearer picture of the reasonableness of the classical, orthodox, protestant, evangelical Christian faith. It is just such a "reasonable faith"[17] that has the power to change lives and in turn, impact our society for the better.

Letter to a Christian Nation: Counter Point

As INTELLIGENT theists and atheists, there are several incontrovertible views we hold in common. First, we agree that we cannot both be right about the tenets of Christianity. We also agree that "to be a true Christian is to believe that all other faiths are mistaken, and profoundly so."[18] Further, we agree that either God exists, or He doesn't. In short, the fundamental laws of logic, like the law of non-contradiction[19], apply to all of us, regardless of our belief system or worldview. Areas of agreement certainly exist between us. However, we also have many areas of disagreement. One of the most glaring of these lies with the presumption that "every devout Muslim has the same reasons for being a Muslim that [I] have for being a Christian."[20] Your assumption leads you to believe that it is valid to compare Islam with Christianity. You state that "Muslims are not making claims about reality that can be corroborated,"[21] and imply the same about Christianity, yet your latter assumption is mistaken.

Throughout your *Letter* you express your fears of religion as the "Root of All Evil"[22] in the world. In your opinion freedom from religion, or should I say *The End of Faith*,[23] would almost certainly entail freedom from terrorism and most wars. In both your books, you list numerous worldwide conflicts between faith-based warring factions. Yet you address your letter to *American Christians.* Do you see American Christians at war with other faiths? Are protestant Christians killing Roman Catholics in the United States due to doctrinal differences? Do you see American Christians diverting air traffic toward buildings in the Middle East? Perhaps you should have addressed your *Letter* to radical Muslims, although we both know it wouldn't sell in the Middle East and a market that comprises less than 1% of Americans would hardly warrant such an edition here in the States.

You state that "questions of morality are questions about happiness and suffering. This is why you and I do not have moral obligations toward rocks."[24] I would suggest that questions of morality spread way beyond the confines you have placed upon them. In a sense, we even have moral obligations toward rocks. Don't we have moral obligations toward sustaining the resources of our earth? Most atheists would say we do. In fact, and this may surprise you, so would most Christians. Theologians include the responsibility of caring for the earth and the environment in what we call the creation mandate.[25]

The orthodox Christian perspective deems it morally proper to express concern over civil rights abuses in other countries and try to aid those countries in bringing such inhumane activity to an end. A president, who grounds his morality in the teachings of Jesus Christ, could not ignore the cruelty reflected in the crimes against humanity that Saddam Hussein inflicted upon his own people. I reside in a city with a high percentage of military personnel. Support for President George W. Bush and the Iraq War started out strong. It has since waned only due to the inability of Americans to clearly see a resolution to the situation in Iraq. Nevertheless, the Christians I've spoken to in our Armed Forces have made a firm commitment to attain stability in Iraq prior to the significant troop withdrawal needed to end the war. A liberal Epicurean or Utilitarian perspective (as I will address later in this book) warrants no real concern over abuses occurring in foreign lands. Both perspectives revert back to the logic that what is best for the individual or local group should prevail and ultimately ignores the needs of outsiders.

♦ ♦ ♦ ♦ ♦ ♦ ♦

Old Testament Laws

YOU MAKE THE unwarranted assumption that many of
the Old Testament laws continue to bind Christians
today. If true, shouldn't we have heard of instances
where Christians acted upon these laws? Wouldn't
home schooling moms kill children frequently for
talking back to them? Wouldn't Andrea Yates, who
drowned her five children in Texas in 2001, have considered first an appeal to Leviticus rather than an
insanity plea? The only place where these laws apply
within today's culture is within certain Jewish sects,
who contend that the Halakha (Jewish religious law)
along with its 613 Commandments, including many
of the ones you cited, should still require strict obedience. Among the vast majority of modern American
Jews a person only binds himself to the Halakha by his
own volition, a choice few actually make. Even among
Orthodox and Haredi Jews, the most conservative seg-
ments of Judaism, the death penalty has been done
away with since the destruction of the Temple in
Jerusalem in 70 AD.

In describing these Old Testament laws and their
penalties, ostensibly to affirm their validity in
American Christianity, you make it a point to cite ref-
erences to the New Testament as well. However your
citations from Matthew 15:4-7 and Mark 7:9-13 refer

only to instances when Jesus alludes to the same Old Testament laws. Both gospel writers explicated the same incident. Jesus spoke to a group of Jewish Pharisees who had already relaxed the penalties of the Old Testament law by rationalizing away the need to care for their parents in their old age. He showed them the hypocrisy of allowing their followers to ignore their obligations to their parents so as to contribute to the Temple. And yes, Jesus actually supported the Law by His words. You confirm this as well by quoting Matthew, which I will repeat here.

> *I tell you the truth, until heaven and earth disappear, not the smallest letter, not the least stroke of a pen, will by any means disappear from the Law until everything is accomplished. Anyone who breaks one of the least of these commandments and teaches others to do the same will be called least in the kingdom of heaven, but whoever practices and teaches these commands will be called great in the kingdom of heaven. For I tell you that unless your righteousness surpasses that of the Pharisees and the teachers of the law, you will certainly not enter the kingdom of heaven.*
>
> —Matthew 5:18-20

However, your quote failed to include the critical verse that preceded these words.

> *Do not think that I have come to abolish the Law or the Prophets; I have not come to abolish them but to fulfill them.*

> —Matthew 5:17

Woven into this one verse we discover the sine qua non ... the summum bonum of the Christian faith. Jesus' purpose here on earth was to fulfill the law, not only by living in total obedience to the law, but also by paying the penalty incurred by everyone who has ever lived or will ever live, who are drawn to place their trust in Him. Paul wrote, "If we claim to be without sin, we deceive ourselves and the truth is not in us."[26] Jesus was the only person who could unequivocally make such a claim.

♦   ♦   ♦   ♦   ♦   ♦   ♦

Original Sin

I AM SURE you will disagree with Paul's statement, since you limit your view of morality to those actions that promote happiness or ease human suffering. Here the Christian doctrine of original sin enters the picture. Richard Dawkins in *The God Delusion* asks "What kind of ethical philosophy is it that condemns every child, even before it is born, to inherit the sin of a remote ancestor?"[27] I suspect you'd ask much the same question. What I find interesting about Dawkins' query is his apparent incognizance of the concepts it entails. Notice his use of the word "inherit." While primarily applied to the field of genetics, I don't find its use inappropriate here. We are not all born with the burden of Adam's specific sin pressing down upon us. Rather, we are each born with an inherent tendency toward sinful behavior; a sense of selfishness that yields a desire to promote our own personal happiness. Contrary to always being morally virtuous, most of us would categorize such behavior as sinful at times, even if only in the sense that, in the process, we may cause suffering to others. From the moment of our birth, we exhibit selfish behavior. But, you may argue, don't all babies disturb their mothers by crying in order to be fed? Isn't this behavior morally neutral? Isn't this simply a necessity that assures our survival? Yes, yet this same tendency toward selfishness, that assures our survival past infancy, causes one child to hurt another simply to obtain a coveted toy. Suddenly, what originally simply promoted our personal happiness has become a means by which we promote human suffering.

Does this mean we have original sin built into our genetic makeup? I'd suggest that since the time of Adam's fall, it has been. Remember, almost 98% of the DNA in the human genome geneticists still classify as "junk DNA,"[28] which may imply a purely structural function or an encoding function that has not yet been identified. Does this mean that we may eventually isolate a single "sin gene"? Perhaps, but for theological reasons, I suspect not. More likely, the "sin trait" has been encrypted within the entire genome, more complex than even a supergene. However, what would better fit the definition of Richard Dawkins' "selfish gene"[29] than a gene for selfishness? A gene that causes an organism to seek its own best interests (i.e. selfishness), even to the point of causing other humans to suffer (i.e. sin), would certainly qualify as a "fit" gene. According to natural selection, such a gene will never be eradicated from the human gene pool.

Richard Dawkins suggests that morality has a Darwinian origin. While evolution has endowed us all with selfish *genes*, this does not imply a selfish organism, selfish group or selfish species.[30] He suggests that four types of altruism have evolved via natural selection. Reciprocal altruism he defines as the 'you scratch my back, I'll scratch yours' type. Kin altruism causes related individuals to 'care for their own.' Third, he presents the altruism that arises when one individual desires to attain a reputation for kindness and generosity. And finally, there is the authentic advertising an individual gains from being conspicuously generous. Of course, Dawkins fails to recognize that none of these examples of "morality" represent classical selfless altruism. In each case, the altruist has a vested self-interest in the action, a self-serving motive. While both you and Dawkins claim that Christians only do good because they believe God is watching everything they do, the atheist version of morality implies that we only do good when there is something "in it for us." Goodness for "goodness' sake" seems a rare commodity in the human species. It's a wonder Santa ever delivers anything but coal!

Promoting one's own happiness and easing human suffering do not always overlap. Granted, if we act altruistically and ease human suffering by helping hurricane victims, this action will likely bring us a sense of personal happiness and accomplishment. However, often times we promote our own happiness at the expense of others. Let's look at another statement you made: "Consider the ratio of salaries paid to top-tier CEOs and those paid to the same firms' average employees: in Britain it is 24:1; in France, 15:1; in Sweden, 13:1; in the United States, where 80 percent of the population expects to be called before God on Judgment Day, it is 475:1." Once again you've adopted the logical fallacy of equivocation and used statistics to your own ends. The New York Review of Books article you cited leaves out the adjectival phrase "where 80 percent of the population expects to be called before God on Judgment Day." The religious affiliations of the American population had nothing whatsoever to do with top-tier CEOs' elections to those positions. Christian values may help someone get elected to political office, but they will have little effect on a CEO making it up the corporate ladder. The number of individuals who comprise that small, select group of CEOs of major companies in America is likely so small that it represents merely a fraction of one percent of even American atheists. The amount of time and energy one has to spend to achieve such a high level position often leaves little time for anything else, like, for instance, religious observance, and frequently causes a bit of human suffering along the way. Do we all inherit original sin? Absolutely. Does this mean that we have no capacity to do good? No, only that we do not have the capacity to *only* do good; we *must* also sin.

The Teachings of Jesus

JESUS TRIED to teach his contemporaries that God created the Law for their benefit. Human beings were not designed to be self-sufficient and live in a state of anarchy. If you prefer, human beings did not evolve[31] to be autonomous. The Law intended to reflect the holiness of God and to strongly impress upon humanity the sort of behavior He deemed moral. As an omniscient God, He knew it wouldn't take long for leniency to ensue. Yet it remained for Him to show mankind that a failure in even one small area of the law equaled a failure in all areas. If all of us today adhered completely to the moral law, as prescribed by God, we could all attain the greatest possible level of personal happiness. Of course, this will never happen on earth as we know it.

Theologians sometimes use Latin terms to express ideas, as do scientists. Theologians would define the state of mankind after Adam's fall as *non posse non peccare* (i.e. not able not to sin). The sinfulness passed down through the gene pool of all mankind affects us all. However, in heaven we will become *non posse peccare* (i.e. not able to sin). Will this occur by a divine restructuring of our genetic material? Perhaps. It is reasonable to consider that, if God exists, He could omnipotently adapt individual components of His creation. However, the most visible means by which he changes individuals and adapts them for heaven, theologians call the process of *sanctification*. Marked by a consistent upward climb, like a graph of the growth in stock prices of a growing company, the believer has an increasing passion to live in obedience to God. Failure will occur as part of the growth process, like the occasional dips on a growing stock chart, but repentance will follow, along with the strength to carry on.

Jesus' message left no doubt that under the Law the penalty for sin is death. Paul spelled out the relationship between the Law and sin in his letter to the Romans.

> *Therefore, just as sin entered the world through one man, and death through sin, and in this way death came to all men, because all sinned—for before the law was given, sin was in the world. But sin is not taken into account when there is no law.*

> —Romans 5:12-13

During Old Testament times, the Law became necessary to curtail the curiosity and sin nature of God's people that God knew would result in their misery. In

the New Testament, the Law points the way to forgiveness and salvation from the penalty of sin. Paul
explains this a little further in Romans.

> *But where sin abounded, grace abounded*
> *much more, so that as sin reigned in*
> *death, even so grace might reign through*
> *righteousness to eternal life through Jesus*
> *Christ our Lord.*

—Romans 5:20-21

Every man, woman and child alive is born a slave to
sin, due to the inheritance of a sin nature. However,
the only person capable of overcoming death, Jesus
Christ, paid the penalty for that sin as our substitute.
While the crucifixion may seem barbaric to you, it was
born on the shoulders of God himself. This means
that God not only created and enacted the Law; He
bore the punishment for our crimes (even if we perceive them as mere peccadilloes), entirely in our place.
Christians understand this as Christ's *atonement* for
our sins. He willingly paid the penalty we rightfully
should have paid ourselves. Richard Dawkins finds
this doctrine of the atonement sado-masochistic and
repellant.[32] Yet the atonement forms the core of the
Christian concept of *grace*. This initial act of grace on
Jesus' part promises us forgiveness of sin and opens the

door to a new life of grace. Henceforth we find ourselves no longer slaves to sin. As Paul says,

> *Don't you know that when you offer yourselves to someone to obey him as slaves, you are slaves to the one whom you obey—whether you are slaves to sin, which leads to death, or to obedience, which leads to righteousness?*

—Romans 6:16

But we can define grace as so much more than mere forgiveness of sins. It also provides an entrance into a life in which God actively participates. God, the Holy Spirit, the third member of the Trinity, works in the lives of believers to empower them toward living sanctified lives that reflect the moral teachings of Jesus.[33] No one can truly understand this aspect of the Christian faith short of personal experience. Since you seem convinced that science offers no evidence favoring the existence of God, it will be especially hard for me to convince you that God actively intervenes in the lives of Christians! However, since I will thoroughly address the scientific evidences for God and Christianity in my next book, I would encourage you to await its publication expectantly.

♦ ♦ ♦ ♦ ♦ ♦ ♦

The Moral Teachings of Jesus

The fifth chapter of Matthew, in its entirety, expresses many of Christ's moral teachings. We've already looked at verses seventeen through twenty. Prior to this Matthew recounts Jesus' well-known *Sermon on the Mount*. Let us look for a moment at just the "Blessed …" statements in this discourse.

> *Blessed are the poor in spirit.*
> *Blessed are those who mourn.*
> *Blessed are the meek.*
> *Blessed are those who hunger and thirst*
> *for righteousness.*
> *Blessed are the merciful.*
> *Blessed are the pure in heart.*
> *Blessed are the peacemakers.*
> *Blessed are those who are persecuted*
> *because of righteousness.*

Do these really look like qualities that should cause our society to tremble? To provide a bit of contrast, let us consider the teaching of the Koran.

> *Fight in the cause of Allah those who fight you, but do not transgress limits; for Allah does not love transgressors. And slay them wherever you catch them, and turn them out from where they have turned you out; for tumult and oppression are worse than slaughter; but do not fight them at the Sacred Mosque, unless they (first) fight you there; but if they fight you, slay them.*

> —Koran 2: 190-191

Consider these explicit remarks regarding Jews and Christians (People of the Book):

> *Fight those who do not believe in Allah … nor acknowledge the Religion of Truth, (even if they are) People of the Book, until they pay the Jizya with willing submission, and feel themselves subdued.*

> —Koran 9:29

Lest you think that the lack of belief in God grants you immunity from Allah's wrath:

> *But when the forbidden months are passed, then fight and slay the Pagans wherever you find them, and seize them,*

> *beleaguer them, and lie in wait for them in every stratagem (of war); but if they repent, and establish regular prayers and practice regular charity, then open the way for them: for Allah is oft-forgiving, Most Merciful.*

—Koran 9:5

This section describes Allah as Most Merciful, provided we convert to Islam or live in subservience to Islam. Living at peace with people who hold opposing worldviews is not an option for a conservative Muslim, however it is a mandate for a conservative Christian. In stark contrast to the teaching of the Koran, Jesus taught:

> *You have heard that it was said, 'Eye for eye, and tooth for tooth.' But I tell you, do not resist an evil person. If someone strikes you on the right cheek, turn to him the other also.*

—Matthew 5:38-39

The writer of Hebrews beautifully summarized the Christians' call to holiness.

> *Make every effort to live in peace with all men and to be holy; without holiness no one will see the Lord.*

—Hebrews 12:14

And the apostle Paul wrote:

> *Bless those who persecute you; bless and do not curse. Rejoice with those who rejoice; mourn with those who mourn. Live in harmony with one another. Do not be proud, but be willing to associate with people of low position. Do not be conceited. Do not repay anyone evil for evil. Be careful to do what is right in the eyes of everybody. If it is possible, as far as it depends on you, live at peace with everyone. Do not take revenge, my friends, but leave room for God's wrath, for it is written: "It is mine to avenge; I will repay," says the Lord.*

—Romans 12:14-19

You write, "Many Christians believe that Jesus did away with all this barbarism in the clearest terms imaginable and delivered a doctrine of pure love and toleration. He didn't." However, you fail to recognize that while endorsing the Old Testament Law, he also fulfilled that Law and thereby modified it for all future generations. If you fail to view the Bible historically and in context, you could easily contrast Matthew 5:39 (quoted above) with many of the verses that lay out the Old Testament law and say "See … the Bible contradicts itself." The Internet furnishes many websites that list presumed contradictions in the Bible, but these invariably take a single verse out of context and compare it with another single verse.

Many of the Old Testament laws do not apply to life in modern America. Two entire chapters of Leviticus (13 & 14) examine laws concerning what translators usually call *leprosy*, however this term also includes other diseases such as smallpox and syphilis. Responsibility for assuring sanitary practices and controlling the spread of infectious diseases fell to the priests, guided by God's Law. Today we have the Centers for Disease Control in Atlanta, Georgia, research facilities at the National Institutes of Health, in Bethesda, Maryland and many capable medical professionals rendering these Levitical laws obsolete. Jesus fulfillment of the Law also brings us an updated, if you will, moral code by which we can pattern our lives. Christians today secure guidance from the morality taught through the life and words of Jesus.

◆   ◆   ◆   ◆   ◆   ◆   ◆

Slavery

SLAVERY HAS existed throughout virtually the entire span of human history. Cultural mores have not remained stagnant over the centuries, and attitudes toward slavery have changed along with them. Abolitionist movements were rare prior to the 18th century. We find the most notable and first recorded exception in the Old Testament book of Exodus. The Old Testament laws helped to ascertain the humane treatment of slaves. However, in Egypt the Israelites served primarily as brick builders and were subject to harsh conditions. Moses led approximately 600,000 Israelite men and their families out of bondage in Egypt.

In the British Empire slaves became emancipated in 1834 due to the tireless efforts of men like William Wilberforce and John Newton. As an atheist, Newton had no moral grounding upon which to base any opposition to slavery. He became a servant on a slave ship and received no better than the slaves he served. He then became captain of his own slave ship. Following a tempestuous storm, John Newton experienced the grace of Christian faith, leading him to repudiate his involvement in the slave trade. William Wilberforce worked tirelessly to secure the abolition of slavery in Britain from 1787 until his death in 1833. Several months prior to his death he witnessed the passage of the Slavery Abolition Act by the British Parliament. The British slave trade finally ended due in large part to the indefatigability of Wilberforce and Newton. Wilberforce also lived an ardent evangelical, protestant Christian life, which began just two years prior to devoting his life to the abolition of slavery. The film *Amazing Grace*, released in February 2007, depicts the stories of these two Christian men.

Slavery in colonial America and Britain in the 18th century was fraught with racism and abuse, but in Old Testament Israel, entrance into slavery simply became a necessity for some. No one forced anyone else into slavery. The slave signed a contract agreeing to serve the master's family for a period of 7 years. At the end of this time, the Law required the cancellation of the contract. During the indenture period, the slave was entitled to all the rights of any other family member, except the right of inheritance. The closest modern analogy would be that of an au pair. A slave would certainly perform much more strenuous tasks than the light housework required of an au pair, nevertheless similar interpersonal relationships would develop.

Your reading of the Bible leads you to believe that "every man is free to sell his daughter into sexual slavery—though certain niceties apply."[34]

> *If a man sells his daughter as a servant, she is not to go free as menservants do. If she does not please the master who has selected her for himself, he must let her be redeemed. He has no right to sell her to foreigners, because he has broken faith with her. If he selects her for his son, he must grant her the rights of a daughter. If he marries another woman, he must not deprive the first one of her food, clothing and marital rights. If he does not provide her with these three things, she is to go free, without any payment of money.*
>
> —Exodus 21:7-11

In the days of the Old Testament, when a man sold his daughter as a servant, he allowed her entrance into a marriage covenant in which she approved. A man or his family typically initiated the sequence of steps leading to marriage. The Old Testament custom included the new husband or his family offering a *bride price* to the father of the bride. Not always a monetary payment, this may have taken the form of a gift of something considered valuable. The above passage does not merely offer applicable niceties, but provides laws protecting women who enter into marriage in this manner.

As an example of a family that included servant brides, let us consider the household of Jacob. Jacob had twelve sons whose descendants gave rise to the Twelve Tribes of Israel: Reuben, Simeon, Levi, Judah, Issachar, Zebulun, Dan, Naphtali, Gad, Asher, Joseph and Benjamin.[35] Jacob fell in love with Rachel and desired to marry her. Jacob then met with her father Laban and arranged to become a slave in the household for seven years, in order to earn Rachel's hand in marriage. Unfortunately for Jacob, the custom in Laban's country assumed the firstborn should enter into marriage first. After seven years had elapsed, Jacob was given Leah in marriage instead of Rachel, which angered him. Laban agreed to allow Jacob to marry Rachel after Leah's bridal week had passed, in return for another seven years of labor. Severely smitten, Jacob continued as Laban's slave for another seven years to win the hand of his beloved Rachel. So Jacob and Rachel also married and expanded the family Jacob had already started with Leah. Both Leah and Rachel were given maidservants who also joined Jacob's family. These maidservants, Zilpah and Bilhah, became servant wives to Jacob by their mutual agreement with Leah and Rachel. While Leah bore Jacob six sons, each of his other three wives bore him two sons. Leah also bore a daughter, Dinah. We find this account in Genesis 29 and 30. Jacob treated his wives, Leah and Rachel, and his servant wives, Zilpah and Bilhah, fairly and equitably. Jacob, his wives and their children lived and traveled together as a family unit after Jacob had finished his contract with Laban.

Polygamy was a commonly accepted practice in ancient Israel. By your reasoning it follows that polygamy would continue as the law of the land here in America, too. After all, Christians make up the largest percentage of the religious population in America. If all the Old Testament laws still bound Christians today, Warren Jeffs wouldn't be the only polygamist patriarch making the news. However, Jesus spoke very clearly in favor of monogamy in Matthew's gospel. Once again, the Old Testament law has been abrogated by Jesus' words.

> *Haven't you read that at the beginning the Creator 'made them male and female,' and said, 'For this reason a man will leave his father and mother and be united to his wife, and the two will become one flesh'? So they are no longer two, but one.*

*Therefore what God has joined together,
let man not separate.*

—Matthew 19:4-6

♦   ♦   ♦   ♦   ♦   ♦   ♦

Sex

YOU SUMMARIZE your views of Christianity's attitudes toward sex with the following statement:

> *Your* [the Christian's] *principal concern appears to be that the creator of the universe will take offense at something people do while naked. This prudery of yours contributes daily to the surplus of human misery.*[36]

You seem to arrive at this conclusion primarily in response to the majority Christian consensus on stem-cell research and abortion. Have you ever considered specifically what Jesus had to say about sex? Once again, let us look at the fifth chapter of Matthew's gospel.

You have heard that it was said, 'Do not commit adultery.' But I tell you that anyone who looks at a woman lustfully has already committed adultery with her in his heart.

—Matthew 5:27-28

Jesus' statement definitely sounded new to his audience, a group of Jewish rabbinic teachers known as Pharisees. They had always believed that adultery was only punishable when action followed lustful desire. Jesus turned this thinking on its head by condemning lust outright.

Pornography is a billion dollar industry that depends solely on profit gained from the promotion of lust. You can see why the Christian Right emerges as the most vocal opponent of pornography. Yet why is that the case? Among pornography's most vocal advocates, the Liberal Left fights for its artistic value and proclaims first amendment rights violations toward those seeking to limit its availability. Jesus recognized the degree to which lust denigrates the dignity of human persons.

Yet are humans really worthy of being treated with dignity? If we evolved solely as another mammalian species, like other animals, then should we really expect to be treated with dignity? That presumption reflects an aura of blatant speciesism, an unwarranted preference for our own species. Yet who among us would choose a lifestyle devoid of dignity? We all have an intrinsic sense of dignity as a direct result of what theologians call the *imago dei* (the image of God). We reflect many of the qualities attributed to God in the Bible, such as love, mercy, compassion, and even anger, although Paul warns us not to sin in our anger.[37] Pornography tramples the inherent dignity of humanity by converting individuals into objects. Men who become addicted to pornography often fail in their marital obligations or commit adultery, resulting in human suffering. Many women become involved in pornography for financial reasons or due to boredom. Though this may superficially appear harmless, those women often regret their actions later in life. Further, pornography doesn't just affect adults, it also affects children.

> *Tragically, the world's oldest profession has one of the world's youngest workforces today. Dawn Herzog Jewell, who wrote this month's cover story [in Christianity Today], "Red-Light Rescue", found that millions of preteen and teenage girls are trapped in prostitution, typically earning money for their families or brothel owners.*[38]

Bored homemakers or struggling co-eds comprise only a small percentage of those involved in pornography. As the above quotation indicates, the vast majority also participate in prostitution and human trafficking. In fact, the only form of slavery that still predominates in our day involves trafficking in persons as a direct result of the pornographic industry the Liberal Left so ardently defends.

> *President Bush's National Security Strategy reaffirmed our belief that promoting democracy and human rights is the most effective long-term strategy for ensuring stability. Included in the Strategy's goals for ending tyranny, spreading freedom, and championing human dignity is our commitment to ending human trafficking: "Trafficking in persons is a form of modern-day slavery, and we strive for its total abolition. Future generations will not excuse those who turn a blind eye to it."[39]*

Consider your comments about the human papillomavirus (HPV). I agree with your initial statements that HPV prevails as the most common sexually transmitted disease in the United States. Nevertheless, the rest of your comments lack the depth necessary to truly educate your reader. The term HPV includes over 100 different types of human papillomavirus, some of which do nothing more than cause common skin warts. Only about 30 transmit sexually, causing not only cervical cancer, but also benign genital warts. Of those 30, we place those that endanger lives into a "high risk" category that includes about 10 types of HPV. Let's examine the remainder of your comments.

> *We now have a vaccine for HPV that appears to be both safe and effective. The vaccine produced 100 percent immunity in the six thousand women who received it as part of a clinical trial. And yet, Christian conservatives in our government have resisted a vaccination program on the grounds that HPV is a valuable impediment to premarital sex. These pious men and women want to preserve cervical cancer as an incentive toward abstinence, even if it sacrifices the lives of thousands of women each year.*[40]

The CDC does consider the HPV vaccine (Gardasil) safe and effective, however your claim of 100 percent efficacy and the implication that it will eradicate cervical cancer if used universally, greatly inflates the facts. It does provide 100 percent effectiveness in providing immunity to the **four** types of HPV it is designed to prevent, but is ineffective for at least six known types of high risk HPV. These four types of HPV cause 70 percent of cervical cancer cases. This means that women will still need to undergo yearly Pap tests. Your statement that Christian conservatives "want to preserve cervical cancer" misleads because it implies that a means for the complete eradication of cervical cancer actually exists. The statement "Christian conservatives in our government have resisted a vaccination program" also misleads in that it implies that Christians completely oppose the development and use of the vaccine. In reality Christians only resist a mandatory vaccination program for elementary school-aged children. Consider these comments from July 15, 2006 in the Washington Post made by Peter Sprigg, vice president for policy at the Family Research Council.

> *After extensive study, we and other pro-family groups have concluded that the clear benefits of developing an HPV vaccine outweigh any potential costs. The groups welcoming it include leading conservative pro-family organizations such as*

the Family Research Council, Focus on the Family, Concerned Women for America and the Medical Institute for Sexual Health.... Pro-family groups are united in believing that parents should decide what is best for their children. We oppose any effort by states to make Gardasil mandatory (for example, making it a requirement for school attendance). If use of the vaccine becomes part of the recommended standard of care, and if the federal Vaccines for Children program pays for vaccination of those children whose families cannot afford it, then vaccination should become widespread without school mandates.[41]

♦   ♦   ♦   ♦   ♦   ♦   ♦

Embryonic Stem Cells

YOUR INCOMPLETE view of morality evidently distorts your analysis of embryonic stem-cell research. If we defined "immoral" as only that which causes human suffering, your case may have some merit. Certainly the needs of your "child with a spinal cord injury"[42] are imperative. Yet, is the destruction of a potentially viable human embryo to produce embryonic stem cells truly the best course of action to help this child? Embryonic stem cell research will not likely offer this child any notable advantages over adult stem cell research. While embryonic stem cells do multiply faster than adult stem cells and have been shown to produce some neuronal regeneration, there still exists a significant likelihood that the child's immune system will mount a graft-versus-host response to the foreign cells. Researchers have found that the presence of the protein *nestin* "indicates neural stem cells are much more active than previously believed. Our brain naturally increases the production of stem cells to aid an injured CNS."[43] These naturally produced stem cells only yield structural astrocytes that provide neuronal support rather than the neurons themselves. Studies conducted by Grill and colleagues on rats have shown that concomitant use of neurotrophin 3 (NT-3), stimulates neural stem cells to develop into functional neurons that result in significant improvement in motor skills.[44] Brain derived neurotrophic factors such as NT-3 are proteins that do not have the potential for host rejection associated with the introduction of embryonic stems cells to the site of a spinal cord injury.

In some other medical situations embryonic stem cell lines **may** offer the best hope. Nevertheless, we really have no way of knowing, at this time, how much success researchers will encounter. A similar situation arose in the 1970s and 1980s with the field of gene therapy. Public pronouncements of the expected results of gene therapy research yielded a throng of suffering patients with high expectations. This resulted in a tremendous let-down as researchers encountered the many unexpected technical difficulties inherent in medical research. In 1995, with minimal progress after more than a decade of gene therapy research, the Director of the National Institutes of Health commissioned a review of the field which led to the following pronouncement:

> *Expectations of current gene therapy protocols have been oversold. Overzealous representation of clinical gene therapy has obscured the exploratory nature of the initial studies, colored the manner in which findings are portrayed to the scientific press and public, and led to the widely held, but mistaken, perception that clinical gene therapy is already highly successful. Such misrepresentation threatens confidence in the field and will inevitably*

> *lead to disappointment in both medical and lay communities. Of even greater concern is the possibility that patients, their families, and health providers may make unwise decisions regarding treatment alternatives, holding out for cures that they mistakenly believe are 'just around the corner.*[45]

Already, in the field of embryonic stem cell research, patients have developed high expectations for a very embryonic field of study.

Scientists at Wake Forest University and Harvard University have recently discovered a much less controversial way of harvesting embryonic stem cells. Researchers retrieved "stem cells from amniotic fluid donated by pregnant women and turned them into several different tissue cell types, including liver, brain, and bone.... Harvard stem cell researcher George Daley said that the finding may mean expectant parents could someday freeze amnio stem cells for use in generating replacement tissue in a sick child, without fear of tissue rejection."[46]

You conclude that Christians oppose embryonic stem cell research because "life starts at the moment of conception" and "there are souls in each of these blastocysts."[47] What does the Christian church generally believe with respect to the concept of a "soul"? The majority of Christians typically do believe that "the soul comes into existence at the point of conception either by a direct act of God (creationism) or by transmission from parents (traducianism)."[48] I adhere to the traducian view, which means that I believe the soul passes on from one generation to the next. However, the crux of the mind-body problem does not lie with the origin of the soul within individuals, but rather with the existence of the soul at all. Your apparent mockery of the concept of the soul leads me to believe that you are convinced that "a human person is purely a physical organism, whose emotional, moral, and religious experience will all ultimetely be explained by the physical and biological sciences."[49] We call this monist view of the mind-body problem *reductive physicalism.* Conversely, I believe that we can achieve a greater understanding of the nature of the soul by dispensing with mockery altogether and accepting insights gained via both science and theology.

While the controversy regarding the nature of the soul remains vitally important to the question of the sanctity of life, the issue of inherent human dignity is equally indispensable. Martin Luther King, Jr. understood the Christian concept of the imago dei. His steadfast belief in the inherent dignity of human persons came as a direct result of his Christian faith.

He received the 1964 Nobel Peace Prize for his efforts to promote equlity for persons of all races. Almost two hundred years earlier, the preamble of the U.S. Declaration of Independence referred to the *self-evident truth* that all men were created equal. Yet as a nation, Americans have only recently reached a consensus that supports that self-evident truth with respect to persons of different races. Perhaps it's time we recognize that same self-evident truth with respect to persons at different stages of development.

♦   ♦   ♦   ♦   ♦   ♦   ♦

Evidence and Faith

YOU OFTEN refer to the irrationality of people of faith who believe based upon insufficient evidence. Referring to Christains, you state, "you feel that you are in a position to judge that Jesus is the Son of God, that the Golden Rule is the height of moral wisdom, and that the Bible is not itself brimming with lies. You are using your own moral intuitions to authenticate the wisdom of the Bible."[50] If our moral intuitions and feelings formed the sum total of our evidences in support of Christianity, I would agree that such a faith lacked rational coherence. This resembles the faith of Mormon missionaries who ask you to read from the Book of Mormon until you obtain a sense of warmth and peace that assures you of its truth. This "burning in the bosom" must provide the best evidence the Book of Mormon has going for it, since scientific and archaeological evidence certainly doesn't support its claims. Allegedly, Joseph Smith found the text for the Book of Mormon inscribed on gold plates buried near a hill named Cumorah in upstate New York. Even though Palmyra, NY residents hold a Hill Cumorah Pageant every summer, no archaeological evidence has confirmed the location of such a hill. Nothing has ever been found that substantiates the description of the events at Cumorah described by Brigham Young in his *Journal of Discourses.*

> *When Joseph got the plates, the angel instructed him to carry them back to the hill Cumorah, which he did. Oliver says that when Joseph and Oliver went there, the hill opened, and they walked into a cave, in which there was a large and spacious room. He says he did not think, at the time, whether they had the light of the sun or artificial light; but that it was just as light as day. They laid the plates on a*

table; it was a large table that stood in the room. Under this table there was a pile of plates as much as two feet high, and there were altogether in this room more plates than probably many wagon loads; they were piled up in the corners and along the walls.[51]

You assume that the Christian faith is a "blind leap" into a world filled with contradictions and unwarranted assertions. You seem to think that Christianity's only redemptive quality lies in its ability to make us feel good about ourselves. This is patently false. The historicity of Christianity has both archaeological and historical support. Let us examine briefly just the *recently* discovered archaeological and historical evidence.

In November of 1990, archaeologists recovered the bones of Caiaphas[52], high priest from 18-37 AD, from an ossuary in Jerusalem. The front of the ossuary was beautifully adorned and an inscription on two sides bore the name Yusef bar Caifa in Hebrew. Soldiers took Jesus to Caiaphas the high priest upon his arrest. We find the account of this incident in Matthew 26.

The pool of Siloam, originally thought to have been discovered in the early 1900s, received new interest in late 2004. A sewer crew uncovered stone steps about 200 yards from the original pool that piqued the interest of archaeologists.[53] The pool had historic significance as a public bath to allow washing before entrance into the Temple, but for years, people have wondered how the original small and narrow pool might have served this purpose. The newly found pool measures 225 ft. along one side, forming a rectangle with tiered steps leading into it. Biblically, the pool served as the site where Jesus' healed a man blind since birth.[54]

I would also like to mention several other notable archaeological discoveries. The beginnings of David's Palace[55] have been found in Jerusalem. (2 Chronicles 8:11) While digging in Gath, the home of the Philistine warrior Goliath, archaeologists have uncovered a shard of pottery inscribed with two Proto-Semitic renderings of the name "Goliath."[56] (1 Samuel 17:4) In Megiddo, in Northern Israel, while extending an Israeli prison, workers uncovered a beautiful mosaic floor bearing the inscription "built in honor of Jesus Christ the God."[57] Discoveries such as these provide support for the accuracy of the biblical texts as historical narratives and also attest to the existence of Jesus and the prevailing view of his divinity among early Christians.

Most intellectual atheists do not struggle with Christianty over this sort of evidence. Nevertheless, it is important for the reader to note that such evidence does exist. You would classify this sort of evidence as "soft" science. Instead, the majority of atheists reject Christian claims that appeal to the supernatural as utterly implausible. When it comes to "hard" scientific evidence for these sorts of claims, Christianity has admittedly fallen short. However, that shouldn't surprise us when individuals with a Christian worldview are routinely passed over for research professorships at major colleges and universities. Atheism has surreptitiously infiltrated our higher educational system. This past year, Dr. Francis Beckwith of Baylor University almost lost a tenure track position in Philosophy, specifically due to his Christian worldview. When major universities seek applicants for positions in the "hard" sciences, they don't favor applicants who espouse a Christian worldview. Each department forms a search committee composed of members of that department, most of whom have never seriously considered Christian truth claims. This might explain why membership in the National Academy of Sciences is 93 percent atheist, as you point out.[58] Christians are subconsciously dissuaded from hard science majors unless they attend a Christian Liberal Arts college. I went through just this sort of struggle twenty-five years ago at a major secular university. While working on my Masters Degree, I was fortunate to have an advisor who respected my opinions and supported my right to disagree with him. Had I been at another school, where my views were ridiculed, rather than respected, I may have left the sciences altogether. I might add that this man always worked on Christmas day, but took the day off for Darwin's birthday. We represented two completely opposing viewpoints yet found it possible to work together in harmony.

♦   ♦   ♦   ♦   ♦   ♦   ♦

So Are Atheists Evil?

MY SHORT RESPONSE would be, "No … and yes." However, I would offer the same answer if you asked "Are Christians evil?" My answer applies to all people. In the sense that both atheists and Christians generally can live good lives (i.e. they become useful members of society, care for their children, etc.), my answer would be "no." However, when we consider inherent human tendencies toward selfish behavior, sometimes at the expense of others, I know of no one who is completely free from such evil.

Many Christian theists have concluded that the existence of evil can provide good evidence for the existence of God. Consider the argument put forth by Ravi Zacharias in his book *A Shattered Visage: The Real Face of Atheism.*[59] In the appendix he writes:

1. *Yes, there is evil in this world.*
2. *If there is evil, there must be good (a problem the atheist has to explain).*
3. *If there is good and evil, there must be a moral law on which to judge between good and evil.*
4. *If there is a moral law, there must be a moral law giver.*
5. *For the theist, this points to God.*

An atheist might respond[60] that proposition number three lacks merit since the only requirement is a moral system, not necessarily a moral law. A moral system may just as easily arise via memetic[61] evolutionary mechanisms as by an omniscient lawgiver. While the existence of memes remains highly speculative, I would grant such a possibility exists.

However, this fails to account for the sort of evil that defies cultural explanation. In most of the section that follows this question in your book, you cite examples such as Adolf Hitler, Kim Il Sung, and Josef Stalin. Humanity world-wide would decry many of the horrors perpetrated by Josef Mengele under the Nazi regime. Mengele injected chemicals into the eyes of infants in an attempt to change their eye color. This experimentation caused severe pain and often permanent blindness. The Third Reich apparently sanctioned such cruelty. It would seem that what one culture considered acceptable would be considered evil in most other cultures. While atheists have done little to stem the tide of cultural evil, Christian missionaries brave the front lines. The Maori of New Zealand practiced cannibalism until 1840, an evil renounced by the Maori in large part due to the evangelistic efforts of Christian missionaries.

> *Missionaries, however, from various Christian churches came to evangelize the heathen. They made a direct attack against the Maori form of theology. The golden rule of brotherly love was preached, and war and cannibalism were condemned. The new religion was accepted by the chiefs, and their tribes followed. It was some time, however, before the various tribes would give up the satisfaction of*

> *using their newly acquired firearms against their hereditary enemies. Old scores had to be settled as a point of tribal honour. Finally, the new teaching prevailed and inter-tribal wars ended. With the cessation of wars, the supply of slain enemies ended and cannibalism ceased.*[62]

We need to recognize that there actually **are** evils in the world that every sane person would abhor. We don't pass laws that specifically say not to put needles into the eyes of little babies. There are evils that we all know, deep down, are truly evil, regardless of one's cultural setting. Yet from where does this knowledge arise? Memetic evolution cannot account for it. This innate level of discernment between good and evil Christians would render as necessarily from God.

Both you and Richard Dawkins seem to believe that evangelical Christianity represents one of the world's worst inherent evils. Dawkins asks, "How much do we regard children as being the property of their parents? Its one thing to say people should be free to believe whatever they like, but should they be free to impose their beliefs on their children? Is there something to be said for society stepping in? What about bringing up children to believe manifest falsehoods?"[63] Yet absolutely no evidence exists to support the claim that Christianity is a manifest falsehood. In fact, Dawkins theory of the existence of memes has as much, if not more, potential for being a manifest falsehood as does the God hypothesis.

In the final analysis, Christian theism, based on the morality of Jesus Christ, provides the most foundationally coherent grounding for morally upright behavior. Such behavior is completely consistent with the teachings of Jesus. Muslim theism offers no such grounding. The teachings of the Koran encourage fighting and violence, as I have shown and as you so often point out. The atheist also has no grounding for morally upright behavior, since evolution alone cannot account for an innate human awareness of right and wrong. Does this mean that atheists and Muslims cannot live moral lives? Absolutely not. Only that their worldviews offer no intrinsic warrant for such behavior.

◆   ◆   ◆   ◆   ◆   ◆   ◆

The Problem of Evil

YOU STATE THAT "an atheist is a person who believes that the murder of a single little girl—even once in a million years—casts doubt upon the idea of a benevolent God." This sounds reasonable. Many Christians have similar doubts when faced with tragic events in the world or in their own lives. You comment, "It is safe to say that almost every person living in New Orleans at the moment Hurricane Katrina struck shared your belief in an omnipotent, omniscient, and compassionate God." While obviously an exaggeration, apparent gratuitous evil is witnessed during natural catastrophes and begs for an explanation. Unfortunately, you will not accept the explanation Christians usually proffer, since it assumes the existence of God. Nevertheless, I will address this issue for the reader's benefit.

We do not contest the existence of evil in the world. Yet, what is evil? In simplest terms, evil is to good as cold is to heat. Heat is a form of energy. The lack of heat energy we experience as cold. Similarly, evil is a privation of good. In order to create a world that would allow humanity the freedom to choose between good and evil, God had to allow the consequences of those evil actions to ensue. An example of this would be the 2001 drought in Sudan. The Khartoum government interfered with UN relief efforts so as to result in a higher rate of death among their own people. While a natural disaster initiated the problem in the Sudan, human choices led to unconscionable consequences. When Hurricane Katrina devastated New Orleans you wrote "God told no one of his plans." Yet you have no way of knowing the truth of your statement. God very well may have worked instrumentally in the lives of many of his people to lead them to avoid this catastrophe. What God did *not* do was interject a spot on the five o'clock news warning the world of His plans.

While some cataclysmic events in nature may be direct, causal "acts of God," others very well may be necessary by-products of the creation of a world suitable for life. Plate tectonics, while resulting in earthquakes and volcanoes, also play a role in the development of petroleum deposits. The water cycle brings us flash flooding and storms, but also distributes water to crops and cattle. The assumption that God could have created a world free of natural catastrophes if truly benevolent requires a level of omniscience only properly His.

♦   ♦   ♦   ♦   ♦   ♦   ♦

Science and Christianity

STEPHEN JAY GOULD, in his 1999 book *Rock of Ages*, coined the term *non-overlapping magisteria* (NOMA) in an attempt to finally resolve the conflict between science and religion. He claimed that scientists had one set of tools that equipped them to study science and answer questions relevant to their domain of science. Theologians were similarly equipped to answer an entirely different set of questions. Since the scientific domain, or magisterium, and the theological magisterium studied a different set of questions, they needn't overlap.

> *The magisterium of science covers the empirical realm: what the Universe is made of (fact) and why does it work in this way (theory). The magisterium of religion extends over questions of ultimate meaning and moral value. These two magisteria do not overlap, nor do they encompass all inquiry (consider, for example, the magisterium of art and the meaning of beauty).*[64]

While this may sound like a pleasing solution to the problem, the fact remains that many of the questions faced by science and religion actually *do* overlap. You most likely would agree with Richard Dawkins when he says, "God's existence or non-existence is a scientific fact about the universe, discoverable in principle if not in practice."[65] Dawkins, however, makes it very clear that he believes that God's existence is *not* discoverable in practice. Of course, if no one who would even remotely consider the God hypothesis is engaged in research at most of our academic institutions of higher learning, God's existence as a scientific fact will likely *never* be postulated. This does not mean that it *cannot* be postulated; only that such a consideration will have to wait until such time as science and theology can complement one another in the search for ultimate truth.

Secularists claim that the God hypothesis does nothing other than put an end to scientific inquiry. They assume that God is only used to fill in the answers to the questions that scientific knowledge hasn't yet discovered. However, I would contend that such a *God of the gaps* mentality is **not** a legitimate use of the God hypothesis. Rather, the biblical God has very explicit attributes that may be explainable scientifically. Certain events documented historically in the Bible may be subjected to scientific evaluation. However, scientific materialism places detour signs that block potentially open roads of scientific inquiry into these arenas.

All too often you revert to discussing "religion" as opposed to Christianity. The title of your section *The Clash of Science and Religion* provides just one example. In contrast, I will make clear the distinction between Christianity and other faiths you so freely subsume under the rubric "religion." Christian orthodox belief, as construed for centuries in the tradition of the Protestant Reformation, makes some distinct claims about the nature and attributes of God that should be subject to scientific scrutiny. Francis Collins, head of the Human Genome Project believes that, "If God exists, then He must be outside the natural world and therefore the tools of science are not the right ones to learn about Him."[66] In contradistinction to Dr. Collins, I would suggest that while the essence of God Himself exists outside the physical universe, Christian claims about God *can* be addressed scientifically. Yet these claims will never be addressed scientifically given the current adversarial climate that exists between scientists and theologians. Your solution is to put an end to all religions. Since so many religions have proven themselves detrimental to society, you assume that none of them has any merit. Yet I would challenge you to put that assumption to the test. We agree that not all religions are true, but this doesn't prove the falsity of every religion. It is possible that *one* religion is actually true. May I suggest that the reason Christianity represents the dominant faith in America today is because so many Americans have already put other religions (and atheism) to the test and found them wanting? Orthodox, evangelical Christianity has found support from soft sciences like archaeology, history and philosophy. Christianity should be put to the test in the hard sciences as well.

◆　◆　◆　◆　◆　◆　◆

Prayer

YOU HAVE THE tendency to scoff at the suggestion that God might actually answer the prayers of His people. You write:

> *What was God doing while Katrina laid waste to their city? Surely He heard the prayers of those elderly men and women who fled the rising waters for the safety of their attics, only to be slowly drowned there. These were people of faith. These were good men and women who had*

> *prayed throughout their lives. Do you*
> *have the courage to admit the obvious?*
> *These poor people died talking to an*
> *imaginary friend.*[67]

Richard Dawkins also takes delight in emphasizing the impotency of prayer. He states that Francis Galton, Charles Darwin's cousin, made the first attempt to scientifically analyze whether or not prayer had any real effect. "He noted that every Sunday, in churches throughout Britain, entire congregations prayed publicly for the health of the royal family. Shouldn't they, therefore, be unusually fit, compared with the rest of us ..." Galton discovered that, statistically, no difference existed between the health of the royal family and the health of the rest of Britain.

We should also note that Francis Galton coined the term *eugenics,* which featured prominently in the rhetoric of Nazi Germany. Galton wrote:

> *We greatly want a brief word to express the*
> *science of improving stock, which is by no*
> *means confined to questions of judicious*
> *mating, but which, especially in the case of*
> *man, takes cognisance of all influences*
> *that tend in however remote a degree to*
> *give to the more suitable races or strains of*

> *blood a better chance of prevailing speedily*
> *over the less suitable than they otherwise*
> *would have had. The word eugenics*
> *would sufficiently express the idea.*[68]

While Galton's pioneering of the failed field of eugenics had no impact on the validity of his study of prayer, the reader may find the above sidebar interesting considering its huge impact on the events of World War II.

Richard Dawkins describes a study funded by the Templeton Foundation designed to experimentally test the effect of prayer on cardiac patients. They performed a double blind study using over 1800 patients, "all of whom received coronary bypass surgery."

> *The patients were divided into three*
> *groups. Group 1 received prayers and did-*
> *n't know it. Group 2 (the control group)*
> *received no prayers and didn't know it.*
> *Group 3 received prayers and did know it.*
> *The comparison between Groups 1 and 2*
> *tests for the efficacy of intercessory prayer.*
> *Group 3 tests for possible psychosomatic*
> *effects of knowing that one is being prayed*
> *for.*[69]

Congregants in three different churches all located hundreds of miles away from the subjects of their prayers, each received the first name and last initial of each of the patients for whom they were to pray, and were told to include the phrase 'for a successful surgery with a quick, healthy recovery and no complications.' The study resulted in no significant difference between the groups who received prayer and the group that didn't receive prayers.

Could such an experiment have any real flaws? What constitute prerequisites of acceptable prayer from God's perspective? The eminent Princeton theologian of the late nineteenth century, Charles Hodge, offered seven criteria.

1. Sincerity—"God is a Spirit. He searches the heart.... He cannot be deceived and will not be mocked.... Everyone must acknowledge ... with regard to the multitudes who, in places of public worship, repeat the solemn forms of devotion or profess to unite with those who utter them, without any corresponding emotions, the service is little more than mockery."

2. Reverence—"Nothing is more characteristic of the prayers recorded in the Bible, than the spirit of reverence by which they are pervaded."

3. Humility—"This includes, first, a due sense of our … uncleanness in the sight of God as sinners."

4. Importunity—"God deals with us as a wise bene-factor. He requires that we should appreciate the value of the blessings for which we ask, and that we should manifest a proper earnestness of desire. If a man begs for his own life or for the life of one dear to him, there is no repressing his importunity."

5. Submission—"Every man who duly appreciates his relation to God, will, no matter what his request, be disposed to say, 'Lord, not my will but thine be done.'"

6. Faith—"We must believe. (a.) That God is. (b.) That He is able to hear and answer our prayers. (c.) That He is disposed to answer them. (d.) That He certainly will answer them, if consistent with his own wise purposes and with our best good."

7. Asking in the name of Christ—"Our Lord said to His disciples 'Hitherto have ye asked nothing in my name: ask, and ye shall receive.'[70] To act in the name of anyone is often to act by his authority, and in the exercise of his power.… When one asks a favour in the name of another, the simple mean-ing is, for his sake. Regard for the person in whose name the favour is requested, is relied on as the ground on which it is to be granted."[71]

How much sincerity is involved in repeating the same line over and over for many people? How importune were the prayers of the congregants when they were unaware of even the surnames of those for whom they were praying? Prayer, by its nature, is a very personal experience. The attempt to statistically analyze the effectiveness of prayer is doomed from the outset. Too many factors lie beyond the control of scientific experimentation.

You seem to find it unconscionable that God "could concern Himself with something as trivial as gay marriage or the name by which He is addressed in prayer …"[72] Yet, suppose you took a class in which a significant portion of the grade depended upon class participation. Let's say fifty people take the class and the professor asks questions of specific individuals that lead into short class discussions. The professor has a system of asking ten questions per class of various people at random and grading their responses. Short discussions follow each question, and you avidly participate. However, you are unaware that the grades are based upon the initial answers. Worse yet, you do not realize that the professor has your name wrong in his grade book. Rather than Sam Harris, he has Saul Morris! Every time he directs a question to Saul Morris he gets no response. You assume this guy should have dropped the course weeks ago. Unfortunately, when the grades come out, you will hardly think it trivial that the professor got your name wrong.

Prayer is not meaningless babble to an "imaginary friend," as you suppose. The active participation of God in the life of a Christian becomes more apparent throughout the life of that Christian. "God's ultimate will is unchanging, but the way in which He chooses to realize this will is dependent on the prayers of his children"[73] Prayers do actually seem to change the apparent course of events in the lives of believers. Does this mean that God constantly changes His mind? No. Rather, He is aware of the changes that take place, and their effects, before they happen. They only appear to us as changes because we do not have His omniscient perspective.

♦   ♦   ♦   ♦   ♦   ♦   ♦

Prophecy

YOU ASK, "How difficult would it have been for the Gospel writers to tell the story of Jesus' life so as to make it conform to Old Testament prophecy?"[74]

While this may appear simple to you, neither the writers, nor any individuals prior to them who may have known Jesus' family personally, had the ability to direct the events of, say, Jesus' birth, in such a way as to convince both Joseph and Mary that this was a normal birth. You claim, with respect to the virgin birth, that Luke and Matthew "relied upon the Greek rendering of Isaiah 7:14. The Hebrew text of Isaiah uses the word *'almâ*, however, which simply means 'young woman,' without any implication of virginity."[75]

> *Therefore the Lord himself will give you a sign: The virgin will be with child and will give birth to a son, and will call him Immanuel.*

—Isaiah 7:14

The Hellenistic ruler of the Egyptian Ptolemaic Empire, Ptolemy II Philadelphus of Alexandria commissioned the Greek rendering of the Hebrew Scriptures in the 260s BC, quite some time before the birth of Christ. The translators were a group of seventy-two Jewish Rabbis, six elders from each of the twelve tribes of Israel,[76] all highly respected for their work. The non-Christian historian Josephus and the ancient philosopher Philo both ascribed divine inspiration to the translators of the Septuagint.

The Dead Sea Scrolls found in Qumran in 1947 included many fragments that agreed closely with the Septuagint, attesting to its place of honor among ancient translations. One of the scrolls found in Qumran also contained "a complete manuscript of the Hebrew text of Isaiah. It is dated by paleographers around 125 BC."[77]

> *The Hebrew word in the text that is translated virgin is "almah." It has a definite article in Hebrew as can be seen in the last word in the first line in the Hebrew text above. It is "ha'almah" or literally "the virgin." Only after the beginning of the Christian dispensation did Jewish scholars insist that the word means a young woman who is not necessarily a virgin and therefore they say a virgin birth was not predicted. Irenaeus is the first one to answer that argument and his points have not been improved upon. One of the most telling arguments he uses is that the Septuagint translators not only translated the verse here but they told what it meant, to them, before the advent of Jesus.[78]*

The Septuagint authors translated the Hebrew word *'almâ* into the Greek work *parthenos,* strictly translated "virgin." Note also that the verse indicates that a *sign* would be given. Most would not consider such a common event as a "young woman giving birth" a *sign*. However, the uniqueness of a virgin giving birth would deem the event worthy of such a designation.[79]

♦   ♦   ♦   ♦   ♦   ♦   ♦

The Legacy of Epicurus

THE MOST INTERESTING aspect of your moral philosophy of happiness sans suffering is its familiarity. I detect an implied hedonism in many of your comments. I don't sense that you would agree with the Cyrenaics, who sought personal pleasure above all, especially sensual pleasures. They believed no benefit could be gained from logic or mental cogitation. The only knowable reality in Cyrenaicism was empirically recognized via the five senses. The Roman emperors Tiberius and Caligula sought this reality to an extreme. Epicureans still sought pleasure, but they recognized that the uncontrolled pursuit of pleasure often led to a decrease in pleasure later in life. They made it their goal to pursue pleasure in moderation. They also recognized that pleasure could be attained by gaining knowledge, a form of pleasure that the Cyrenaics rejected.

As a teenager Epicurus read frequently the works of Democritus, a pre-Socratic philosopher and scientist who, along with Leucippus, constructed a theory of nature strikingly similar to that of early twentieth-century science. In the 3rd and 4th centuries BC, Democritus and Leucippus described nature as composed of atoms, the smallest indivisible unit of matter. They considered all of nature to be composed of either atoms or vacuous space. Since these fundamental components of nature existed eternally, no need existed to include a concept of God. Democritus was a strict materialist, whose philosophy, developed from his scientific theories, parallels the philosophical views of most scientists today.

> *Democritus developed a very lofty set of rules for human behavior, urging moderation in all things along with the cultivation of culture as the surest way of achieving the most desirable goal of life, namely, cheerfulness.*[80]

"Epicurus thought that he had liberated man from the fear of God and from the fear of death."[81] Since death merely represented the cessation of natural existence, and the atoms that comprised humans no longer functioned, no pain or suffering could exist after death. What you're trying to accomplish today by putting an end to faith, Epicurus already attempted over 2300 years ago!

Of course, if Epicurus had wholly eradicated faith in his time, we would be living in a completely secular culture today. Obviously, faith lived on. Within Epicurus' sphere of influence an atheistic moral philosophy freely developed. His moral emphasis "focused upon the individual and his immediate desires for bodily and mental pleasures instead of upon abstract principles of right conduct or consideration of God's commands."[82] Individual happiness became the guiding principle of human morality. Epicurus recognized that we all have a clear sense of the difference between pain and pleasure, and that we view pleasure as by far the more desirable. Hence, Epicurus' philosophy focused on the avoidance of pain and the accrual of pleasure. Unlike the Cyrenaics, Epicurus recognized that a lifetime of pleasure would not come from drunken revelry and the unconstrained satisfaction of lust. He opted for a more moderate stance that avoided overindulgence. Yet, ultimately, like the Cyreniacs, the Epicureans lived as hedonists with a moral philosophy of self-absorption. They avoided concern for the needs of the poor and societal troubles unless they happened to impinge upon their individual happiness in some way. "The only function of civil society that Epicurus would recognize was to deter those who might inflict pain upon individuals."[83] The comparison between your morality and Epicureanism may fail if you truly do have a concern for the welfare of others, even those unknown to you. However, it succeeds in that neither you nor Epicurus has any warrant or rational impetus for such concern.

Perhaps you prefer the utilitarianism of John Stuart Mill or Peter Singer. On Singer's philosophy, you can never attain personal happiness unless you have something to be happy about, and one such focus should include your desire to increase the personal happiness of others. Unfortunately, this leads to the adoption of the concept of the *greater good*. Such utilitarianism may have argued that the institution of slavery in colonial America benefited more people in society than it harmed, hence it was good. This would have proven especially true for the slave owner. Since there was no way to quantify or measure the degree of pleasure derived by the general population or the degree of displeasure inflicted upon the slaves, the determination of the greater good came down to individual personal happiness. If you asked a utilitarian slave to judge the situation, his response would have differed greatly from the response of the slave owner.

In the last chapter of *The End of Faith* you point out your reluctance to criticize Buddhism, professing your proclivity toward Eastern thought. I might suggest that you are drawn to Buddhism, not by its rationality, but because it seems to highlight things you already personally desire, such as peace, love, freedom from suffering and, most of all, no God. Fundamental to Buddhist philosophy, however, we find the concept that we are all *an?tman*, devoid of the self or the soul. This may appeal to you in light of your propensity toward reductive physicalism. However, how do you reconcile the Buddhist view of the 4 Noble Truths with rational western thought? Let me summarize the 4 Noble Truths:

1. *Suffering exists.*
2. *The cause of suffering is desire.*
3. *The end of suffering requires the extinguishing of desire.*
4. *The way to extinguish desire is by following the Eightfold Path.*

I won't delve into the Eightfold Path in this treatise, however, implicit within, one finds the necessity to *desire* freedom from desire. Not only is this intrinsically incoherent, but also utterly discordant with your *desire* to see *The End of Faith*.

In the end, I haven't found a succinct statement of your philosophical beliefs. In *The End of Faith* you stated that, "The notion of a moral community resolves many paradoxes of human behavior."[84] Yet you go on to say that, "The problem of specifying the criteria for inclusion in our moral community is one for which I do not have a detailed answer."[85] Then you get to the crux of your problem and our difference. You state that we cannot simply categorize all humans as part of our moral community and all animals as not. You elaborate further by claiming, "Most of us suspect rabbits are not capable of experiencing happiness or suffering on a human scale. Admittedly we could be wrong about this. And if it ever seems that we have underestimated the subjectivity of rabbits, our ethical stance toward them would no doubt change."[86] Scientifically, almost all animals have pain receptors that cause them to avoid painful circumstances. An electric fence would hardly contain horses or cattle if not viewed as a deterrent. Since we have no way of assessing the happiness of animals, even though they feel pain, on your criteria we could not include them in the community.

How does the notion of a moral community, presumably that group deserving of especially humane treatment, resolve so many paradoxes when you cannot clearly define criteria for inclusion in it? Humanity, by virtue of the imago dei, *is* the only moral community you should seek, and the recognition of the sanctity of *human* life, regardless of subjectivity, Christians hold in the highest regard. Humanity includes humans at the earliest stages of development as well as humans, like Terri Schiavo or Christopher Reeve, who have suffered tragically.

Can you understand now why I mentioned the Cyrenaics earlier? You reserve your concern regarding inclusion in your moral community for any creature capable of experiencing happiness, pain or suffering *now*. In spite of the lifetime of potential human-scale happiness denied an aborted fetus, since they have no ability to suffer *now*, you exclude them from your moral community. Ultimately, if natural selection devoid of God brought us to where we are today, then we would have no one to turn to but ourselves for inclusion criteria. The acceptance of the God hypothesis signifies that the Christian's moral community has already been determined.

◆   ◆   ◆   ◆   ◆   ◆   ◆

Happiness & the Relief of Human Suffering

DO INDIVIDUAL HAPPINESS and the relief of human suffering really represent the supreme expressions of *good* in society today? Are things that cause us happiness as individuals always good for us? Does human suffering ever involve a higher good? Defining morality in terms of happiness and suffering proves too simplistic. For example, many psychotropic drugs cause the user to experience euphoria, an extreme sense of happiness, yet these same drugs can cause physical addiction and organ damage, leading to death over long periods of use. You have stated previously, "When one looks at our drug laws—the only organizing principle that appears to make sense of them is that anything which might radically eclipse prayer or procreative sexuality as a source of pleasure has been outlawed."[87] Most readers will readily see the exaggeration and anti-Christian rhetoric in such a statement. You point out, "In particular, any drug (LSD, mescaline, psilocybin, DMT, MDMA, marijuana, etc.) to which spiritual or religious significance has been ascribed by its users has been prohibited."[88] Like all drugs, even those in regular use, the desired effects come laden with undesirable side-effects that affect members of the population unevenly. LSD, mescaline, psilocybin, dimethyltryptamine (DMT), and Ecstasy (MDMA) are all hallucinogens that offer the user side-effects such as vomiting, diarrhea, tachycardia (increased heart rate), dizziness, headaches, and anxiety. These drugs may also result in a long-term side-effect known as hallucinogen persisting perception disorder (HPPD) that can lead to life-long anxiety issues and sleep disorders. Psychotropic drugs provide instant gratification, but come with a heavy price tag.

While you won't likely have much success convincing your readers that such dangerous street drugs should be legalized, you clearly think that "nearly everything human beings do ... is more dangerous than smoking marijuana in the privacy of one's own home."[89] After all, as you say, "drugs like aspirin and ibuprofen account for an estimated 7,600 deaths each year in the United States alone, [but] marijuana kills no one."[90] While apparently harmless, from your estimation, marijuana has begun to gain recognition for the danger it presents.

Marijuana use is much more dangerous than believed and hundreds of young people die each year in "accidents" caused by their prolonged use of the drug, according to Britain's most senior coroner. Hamish Turner, the president of the Coroners' Society, told The Telegraph that the marijuana, often portrayed as harmless, has increasingly been the cause of deaths that have been reported as accidents or suicides.[91]

While the opinion of one coroner offers only anecdotal support, let's consider what the White House Office of National Drug Control Policy reports.

The Drug Abuse Warning Network (DAWN) collects information on deaths involving drug abuse that were identified and submitted by 128 death investigation jurisdictions in 42 metropolitan areas across the United States. Cannabis ranked among the 10 most common drugs in 16 cities, including Detroit (74 deaths), Dallas (65), and Kansas City (63). Marijuana is very often reported in combination with other substances; in metropolitan areas that reported any marijuana in drug abuse deaths, an average of 79 percent of those deaths involved marijuana and at least one other substance.[92]

What about the concept of human suffering? Is suffering always perceived negatively? Should we avoid it at all costs? Occasionally short-term pain acts as a warning device so that we can avoid long-term suffering. When we experience unexpected physical pain, it can serve as an admonishment that our health may be in jeopardy. If we address this indicator at an early stage, we often can look back and view that pain as a blessing.

♦   ♦   ♦   ♦   ♦   ♦   ♦

Seeking the Truth

CONTRARY TO YOUR DESIRE to see the eradication of all religions, I would prefer to see a greater degree of cooperation between science and theology. I find your claim that all faith-based beliefs are "flagrantly irrational"[93] hopelessly naïve. If the truth claims of various religions were tested scientifically, and the resulting accumulation of evidence favored one religion, its validity would be strengthened. However, if scientists and theologians do not begin to accept such a complimentary approach to the accumulation of knowledge, we will always remain on opposite sides of the fence. We could add the weight of such hard scientific evidence to the weight of existing evidence from the soft sciences, such as that found through archaeology and history.

We clearly cannot conclusively prove any religion wrong due to the impossibility of confirming a universal negative. Suppose I asked myself the question, "Is there enough gold in Alaska to subsidize homes for all the homeless in Seattle?" I could only answer this question in the negative after an exhaustive search of every cubic inch of Alaska. Similarly, I could only affirm the non-existence of God after having searched the entire universe, an impossible task. To answer this question in the positive, I would need to search and find gold nuggets, calculate their value and keep an ongoing tally. Each nugget added to my storehouse would bring me a bit closer to answering the question in the affirmative. Similarly, to affirm the existence of the God of the Bible, I would need to accumulate evidence that adds weight to the argument for His existence.

The archaeological evidence I previously cited provides a few nuggets to add weight to the argument for the validity of Christianity, at least as it relates to the historicity of the biblical manuscripts. The individual testimonies of the life changes attributable to Christian faith provide even more nuggets, although you may disregard these as mere pebbles. If the hard sciences begin to produce evidence for Christianity, this should provide even more weight to the Christian argument. Perhaps such evidence would amount to a gold brick.

In the New Testament, the only sort of evidence available to Jesus' contemporaries was the evidence of the miracles He had performed and the testimonies of those who witnessed these events. Yet neither Jesus nor Luke would deny the impact of evidence or the role of skeptical inquiry on the faith of the believers.

> *Believe me when I say that I am in the Father and the Father is in me; or at least believe on the evidence of the miracles themselves.*
>
> —Jesus in John 14:11

> *Now the Bereans were of more noble character than the Thessalonians, for they received the message with great eagerness*

*and examined the Scriptures every day to
see if what Paul said was true.*

—Luke in Acts 17:11

Most atheists call themselves *freethinkers.* Yet how
can thinking be free if certain areas of knowledge are
summarily excluded as unworthy of cerebration?
Someone truly free should not hesitate to include all
areas of knowledge into their thinking. You claim
that, "We desperately need a public discourse that
encourages critical thinking and intellectual hon-
esty."[94] I couldn't agree more with that statement.
However, I stand in stark disagreement with your
next, which states, "Nothing stands in the way of this
project more than the respect we accord religious
faith."[95] Unfortunately, as I have alluded to previously, that respect doesn't seem to extend within the
hard sciences.

In your conclusion you assert that Christians are
"right to believe that there is more to life than simply
understanding the structure and contents of the universe. But this does not make unjustified (and unjustifiable) claims about its structure and contents any
more respectable." The arrogance and omniscience
required to label another's claims "unjustifiable" does-
n't befit you. Good and rational reasons exist to accept
the validity of Christianity. Nevertheless, I understand

your perspective, having once viewed Christianity in exactly the same way. Now, I can say with John Bradford, the English martyr who died under the reign of Mary I, "There, but for the grace of God go I."

♦   ♦   ♦   ♦   ♦   ♦   ♦

A Personal Reflection

My grandfather worked as an entomologist at Johns Hopkins University and devoted his life to understanding disease-carrying insects, especially mosquitoes. He conferred the name *Anopheles darlingi* on the mosquito of South and Central America most responsible for transmitting malaria to humans. His passion for understanding these disease vectors was only exceeded by his passion to enable others to learn how to control them … and, admittedly, by his passion for my grandmother!

A *scientific realist* prior to the time the term became en vogue, my grandfather believed that his careful documentation and description of *Anopheles* species, embellished by my grandmother's life-like drawings, would help future scientists learn how to decrease the incidence of malaria. Science provided him an objective study of reality that enabled progressive understanding to take place. On realism, philosopher J.P. Moreland notes:

> *[Stanley] Jaki adds that science and natural theology proceed in a similar way—both use a bold leap of the intellect beyond sensory phenomena to the postulation of unseen causes responsible for those phenomena. Thus both natural theology and a realist understanding of science reject crude empiricism and use similar structures in arguments to the best explanation.*[96]

After receiving Bachelors and Masters Degrees in the hard sciences, my father received his Ph.D. in Philosophy from Yale University and worked as the chief technical editor for Johns Hopkins University's Applied Physics Laboratory for over 40 years. During my youth I attended a Unitarian Universalist church in the suburbs of Washington, DC with my family. Sunday school often came down to a choice between arts & crafts or listening to Bible stories depicted in a way that made them analogous to Aesop's *Fables*. I recall standing outside the church at age twelve answering a friend who asked, "Do you believe in God?" At the time I did little more than reiterate my father's beliefs, "Not if the whole Bible is just a bunch of stories!" As a Boy Scout reciting the 12 Scout Laws I always stopped short of the last one, "a scout is reverent." While reciting the Pledge of Allegiance at school I consistently went silent while the rest of the class said "under God." I was a quiet rebel.

At the age of eighteen or nineteen I began to think about religion for myself. What modern atheists call *freethought* led me away from atheism and ultimately to Jesus Christ. In 1975, during my first semester of college, I dated a Christian young lady who encouraged me to read the New Testament as a whole, rather than just jumping from one Bible "story" to the next. Her suggestion helped me to view Jesus Christ and his impact on the world with greater understanding. Although my upbringing had trained me to view everything through the lens of science, I detected more to this Christ than science alone could explain. In December of 1975, my life radically changed due to an awareness of God in Christ that I find difficult to explain to those who haven't experienced a similar event. There were countless theological concepts I had yet to understand. Then again, there were countless scientific concepts I had yet to understand at that age, so I could not rule out the possibility that these two disciplines would not ultimately support one another. For the past thirty years I have sought to deepen my understanding of these issues to determine whether such a synergy is possible. I am convinced it is.

In the meantime my father had become a more outspoken atheist. He retired in the late 1980s and moved to Florida. My parents attended a Unitarian Universalist church at first, but in time the church split and he and some others led an offshoot group to develop a new church based on *Naturalism*. Obviously, my father's worldview differed radically from my own. In late 2003, my 80-year-old father contracted pneumonia and was hospitalized. Although he recovered from the pneumonia, his lungs weakened and he contracted pulmonary fibrosis, which took his life on Father's Day in 2004. During the interval between his hospitalization and his death I gave him a preliminary draft of the manuscript for my next book, tentatively titled *Colliding with Christ: The Science of Resurrection*. I flew from my home in Colorado three times to visit him in Florida during that period. During my last visit he took me aside and whispered, "I think you're right. I really think you're right." This led to a change I had prayed for all my life, but truthfully, did not ever expect to witness. He began to talk about "the transition," a manner of speaking about death that, rather than mere annihilation, expressed a real faith in the reality of heaven. My last conversation with him occurred during a rather one-sided telephone call. His mental faculties remained as sharp as ever, but he found it difficult to both speak and breathe. We spoke for five or ten minutes when suddenly he could speak no more. I spent the next twenty minutes talking to him about his newly found faith. I set down the phone with the final admonition to "Trust Jesus." The next day he died. At the memorial service a few days later my mother inquired, "What did you say to him that night? He would not let go of that phone for over an hour and he appeared more calm and peaceful than I'd seen him in days." I saved my answer to her question until later in the service when I spoke to everyone. As I related our last conversation to the entire congregation of my father's new church, founded on metaphysical naturalism, I offered them the same hope that he had found.

♦　♦　♦　♦　♦　♦　♦

Conclusion

Paul's words in his first letter to the church he helped establish in Corinth, summarize so much of what I have tried to elucidate in this book. The evidence for the veridicality of the Resurrection of Christ is growing. In William Lane Craig's *The Son Rises* he masterfully summarizes the historical and philosophical evidence for the Resurrection. N.T. Wright's voluminous work entitled *The Resurrection of the Son of God* offers an in-depth evaluation of these same arguments and more.

> *For what I received I passed on to you as of first importance: that Christ died for our sins according to the Scriptures, that he was buried, that he was raised on the third day according to the Scriptures, and that he appeared to Peter, and then to the Twelve. After that, he appeared to more than five hundred of the brothers at the same time, most of whom are still living, though some have fallen asleep. Then he appeared to James, then to all the apostles, and last of all he appeared to me also, as to one abnormally born. For I am the least of the apostles and do not even deserve to be called an apostle, because I persecuted the church of God. But by the grace of God I am what I am, and his grace to me was not without effect. No, I*

worked harder than all of them—yet not I, but the grace of God that was with me. Whether, then, it was I or they, this is what we preach, and this is what you believed. But if it is preached that Christ has been raised from the dead, how can some of you say that there is no resurrection of the dead? If there is no resurrection of the dead, then not even Christ has been raised. And if Christ has not been raised, our preaching is useless and so is your faith. More than that, we are then found to be false witnesses about God, for we have testified about God that he raised Christ from the dead. But he did not raise him if in fact the dead are not raised. For if the dead are not raised, then Christ has not been raised either. And if Christ has not been raised, your faith is futile; you are still in your sins. Then those also who have fallen asleep in Christ are lost. If only for this life we have hope in Christ, we are to be pitied more than all men. But Christ has indeed been raised from the dead, the firstfruits of those who have fallen asleep. For since death came through a man, the resurrection of the dead comes also through a man. For as in Adam all die, so in Christ all will be made alive.

—1 Cor. 15:3-22

You probably consider the hope of a life beyond this mortal coil as nothing more than a mere pipe dream. However, millions of Americans see it as a present reality. The atheist has nothing to offer the dying man or woman who struggles with end of life concerns other than the legacy that may continue from the contributions made during his or her lifetime. The atheist offers no solution to the problem of apparent gratuitous evil. If we are all mere products of a Godless form of natural selection, many of us will have little more to look forward to than a life without hope, filled with unexplained suffering and ending in personal extinction. God provides the ultimate solution to the problems of evil and death, for He has offered to every one of us a means of living a life that counts forever and entering into the incommensurable joy of an eternity with Him.

THE END

TEN BOOKS I RECOMMEND

1. *Reasonable Faith* by William Lane Craig

2. *Scaling the Secular City* by J.P. Moreland

3. *The Holiness of God* by R.C. Sproul

4. *The Language of God* by Francis Collins

5. *I Don't Have Enough Faith to be an Atheist* by Norman Geisler & Frank Turek

6. *Walking from East to West* by Ravi Zacharias

7. *God: Coming Face to Face with His Majesty* by John MacArthur, Jr.

8. *The Resurrection of the Son of God* by N.T. Wright

9. *Authentic Christianity* by John R.W. Stott

10. *Classical Apologetics* by R.C. Sproul, Arthur Lindsley and John Gerstner

CONTACT INFORMATION

For more information on Christianity, visit:
www.AllAboutGOD.com

To contact the author, please visit his website at:
www.rcmetcalf.com

NOTES

1   Sam Harris, *Letter to a Christian Nation* (Knopf: New York, 2006), p. vii.

2   Ibid.

3   The word "catholic" refers to the universal group of all true Christians everywhere who comprise the true church, not a specific sect, group or body. When capitalized, this same word is often used to denote the Roman Catholic Church, which excludes all protestant denominations.

4   Specifically in his latest book *The God Delusion*.

5   Sam Harris, Ibid., p. 12.

6   William Manchester *A World Lit Only by Fire* (Little, Brown & Co.: Boston, 1992).

7   Kenneth Scout Latourette *A History of Christianity* (Harper: San Francisco, 1975), p. 759.

8   See Alister McGrath *A Life of John Calvin* (Blackwell Publishing: Oxford, 1993), passim.

9   http://pewforum.org/publications/reports/poll2002.pdf, p. 49.

10   Sam Harris, Ibid, p. viii.

11   Ibid., p. ix.

12   Ibid., p. x.

13   Ibid.

14   http://www.answers.com/topic/islam-in-the-united-states.

15   The phrase "you believe," or something much like it, is used to launch many sections of Harris' *Letter*.

16   Sam Harris, Ibid., p. viii.

17   I would encourage the reader to visit www.reasonablefaith.org, the website of Dr. William Lane Craig, for further insight as to the veridicality of Christianity.

18   Sam Harris, Ibid., p. 3.

19   The law of non-contradiction simply states that something cannot both "be" and "not be" at the same time and in the same relationship. For example, I cannot "be" typing this sentence and "not be" typing this sentence at the same time and in the same relationship.

20   Sam Harris, Ibid., p. 6.

21 Ibid., p. 6,7.

22 This is the title of a documentary hosted by Richard Dawkins that was originally aired on Ch. 4 in the UK. Dr. Dawkins was not entirely pleased with this title since he holds that religion is not the root of *all* evil, just most of it.

23 This is the title of Sam Harris' first book.

24 Sam Harris, Ibid., p. 8.

25 See Genesis 1:26-30.

26 See 1 John 1:8.

27 Richard Dawkins *The God Delusion* (New York: Houghton Mifflin, 2006), p. 253.

28 http://www.ornl.gov/sci/techresources/ Human_Genome/publicat/primer2001/1.shtml and http://www.ornl.gov/sci/techresources/ Human_Genome/glossary/glossary_j.shtml.

29 Richard Dawkins *The Selfish Gene: 30th Anniversary Edition* (London: Oxford University Press, 2006).

30. Richard Dawkins *The God Delusion*, p. 215.

31 My argument here is not with evolution, but I reserve the right to address the issue in the future.

32 Richard Dawkins *The God Delusion*, p. 252.

33 You may think, in light of the failures of prominent men who have laid claim to the Christian faith that this doesn't ring true. Yet for every one fallen Christian leader there are dozens who are continuing to seek righteousness daily. We are not promised complete freedom from sin in this life, only God's help in the struggle. See Romans 7.

34 Sam Harris, p. 15. Ref. Exodus 21:7-11.

35 See Genesis 35:23-26.

36 Sam Harris, p. 26.

37 See Ephesians 4:26.

38 http://www.christianitytoday.com/ct/2007/january/18.10.html.

39 Condoleeza Rice, *Trafficking in Persons Report* (U.S. State Department, June 5, 2006). (http://www.state.gov/g/tip/rls/tiprpt/2006/65982.htm).

40 Sam Harris, p. 26-27.

41 http://www.washingtonpost.com/wp-dyn/content/article/2006/07/14/AR2006071401532_pf.html.

42 Sam Harris, p. 32.

43 http://www.namiscc.org/newsletters/
    December01/SCI-stem-cell-research.htm.
    CNS stands for "central nervous system."

44 Grill, R., Gage, F.H., Murai, K., Blesch, A. &
    Tuszynski, M.H. "Cellular delivery of neu-
    rotrophin-3 promotes corticospinal axonal
    growth and partial functional recovery after spinal
    cord injury" *J. Neuroscience* 17: 5560-5572
    (1997).

45 Shirley M. Tilghman "Address to the Stem Cell
    Institute of New Jersey" (Princeton University:
    November 11, 2004). (http://www.princeton.edu/
    president/speeches/20041111/index.xml),
    (http://www.nih.gov/news/panelrep.html).

46 Lynn Vincent "First Do No Harm" (World
    Magazine: January 20, 2007), p. 30.

47 Sam Harris, p. 31.

48 J.P. Moreland & Scott B. Rae *Body & Soul:
    Human Nature & the Crisis in Ethics* (Downers
    Grove, IL: InterVarsity Press, 2000), p. 205-206.

49 Phil Lueck "What Does It Mean To Be Human?:
    In Search of a Theology of the Soul in an Age of
    Science: Issues, Assumptions, Options, and
    Challenges" (Minneapolis, MN: The MacLaurin
    Institute, 2006). (http://www.maclaurin.org/
    article_print.php?a_id=71).

50 Sam Harris, p. 49.

51 Brigham Young *Journal of Discourses* 19. (http://journalofdiscourses.org/Vol_19/ JD19-036.html).

52 See http://www.bib-arch.org/bswbOOossuary_ Lemaire.pdf.

53 See http://www.bib-arch.org/siloam.pdf.

54 See John 9.

55 See http://www.leaderu.com/theology/palacedavid. html and http://www.archaeologynews.org/ link.asp?ID=73262&Title=Eilat%20Mazar:%20 Uncovering%20King%20David's%20Palace.

56 See http://www.imra.org.il/story.php3?id=27455.

57 See http://www.archaeology.org.il/newsticker.asp? id=24.

58 Sam Harris, p. 39.

59 Ravi Zacharias *A Shattered Visage: The Real Face of Atheism* (Grand Rapids, MI: Baker, 1993), p. 176.

60 Doug Krueger "That Colossal Wreck" (1997), see http://www.infidels.org/library/modern/doug_kr ueger/colossal.html.

61 Memetics refers to the study of "memes." A *meme*, coined by Richard Dawkins in 1976, is

analogous to a gene, in which social and cultural trends are considered analogous to hereditary traits, and evolve over time.

62 Peter H. Buck "Native Races Need Not Die" (National Library of New Zealand, 1952) (http://teaohou.natlib.govt.nz/teaohou/issue/Ma o01TeA/c10.html).

63 http://www.wired.com/news/wiredmag/1,71985-3.html.

64 Stephen Jay Gould *Rock of Ages: Science and Religion in the Fullness of Life* (New York: Ballantine Books, 1999), p. 6.

65 Richard Dawkins *The God Delusion*, p. 50.

66. Francis Collins *The Language of God* (New York: Free Press, 2006), p. 30.

67 Sam Harris, p. 52.

68 Francis Galton *Inquiries into human faculty and its development* (London: Macmillan, 1883): 17, fn1.

69 Richard Dawkins *The God Delusion*, p. 63.

70 John 16:24. See also John 15:16 and John 14:13.

71 Charles Hodge *Systematic Theology: Volume III* (Hendrickson, 2003), p. 701-704.

72 Sam Harris, p. 55.

73   Walter A. Elwell, Ed. Evangelical Dictionary of Theology (Baker Booka: Grand Rapids, 1984), p. 867. See also John 1:12 and 1 John 3:1.

74   Sam Harris, p. 57.

75   Ibid., p. 58.

76   F.F. Bruce *The Books and the Parchments* (Westwood: Fleming H. Revell, 1963), p. 146-147.

77   Josh McDowell *Evidence That Demands a Verdict* (San Bernardino, CS: Here's Life, 1979), p. 58.

78   http://www.ao.net/~fmoeller/7-8.htm#alma.

79   See also http://www.hadavar.org/antimissionary4.html and http://www.asia.si.edu/exhibitions/online/ITB/html/earliestScriptures.htm.

80   Samuel E. Stumpf *Socrates to Sartre 4th Ed.* (New York: McGraw Hill, 1988), p. 28.

81   Ibid., p. 111.

82   Ibid.

83   Ibid., p. 113.

84   Sam Harris *The End of Faith: Religion, Terror and the Future of Reason* (New York: W.W. Norton, 2004), p. 176.

85   Ibid., p. 177.

86   Ibid.

87　Ibid., p. 160.

88　Ibid., pg. 160-161.

89　Ibid., p. 161.

90　Ibid.

91　http://alcoholism.about.com/b/a/039646.htm.

92　Substance Abuse and Mental Health Services Administration, <u>Mortality Data from the Drug Abuse Warning Network, 2001</u> (PDF), January 2003, see http://dawninfo.samhsa.gov/old_dawn/pubs_94_02/mepubs/files/DAWN2001/DAWN2001.pdf.

93　Sam Harris *Letter to a Christian Nation*, p. 87.

94　Sam Harris, p. 87.

95　Ibid.

96　J.P. Moreland, *Christianity and the Nature of Science* (Grand Rapids: Baker Books, 1989), 203; Stanley Jaki, *The Road of Science and the Ways to God* (Chicago: University of Chicago Press, 1978).

978-0-595-43264-6
0-595-43264-6

Printed in the United States
85544LV00001B/136-165/A

9 780595 432646